Rookie Read-About® **Science**

It's a Good Thing There Are
Snakes

by Lisa M. Herrington

Content Consultant
Elizabeth Case DeSantis, M.A. Elementary Education
Julia A. Stark Elementary School, Stamford, Connecticut

Reading Consultant
Jeanne Clidas, Ph.D.
Reading Specialist

Children's Press®
An Imprint of Scholastic Inc.
New York Toronto London Auckland Sydney
Mexico City New Delhi Hong Kong
Danbury, Connecticut

Library of Congress Cataloging-in-Publication Data
Herrington, Lisa M., author.
It's a good thing there are snakes/by Lisa M. Herrington.
     pages cm. — (Rookie read-about science)
Summary: "Introduces the reader to snakes and explains the roles they play in the
environment."— Provided by publisher.
Audience: Ages 3-6.
ISBN 978-0-531-22361-1 (library binding: alk. paper) — ISBN 978-0-531-22833-3 (pbk.: alk. paper)
  1. Snakes—Juvenile literature. I. Title. II. Title: It is a good thing there are snakes.
III. Series: Rookie read-about science.

  QL666.O6H578 2015
  597.96—dc23   2014014969

Produced by Spooky Cheetah Press
Design by Keith Plechaty

Printed in China 62

SCHOLASTIC, CHILDREN'S PRESS, ROOKIE READ-ABOUT®, and associated logos
are trademarks and/or registered trademarks of Scholastic Inc.

1 2 3 4 5 6 7 8 9 10 R 24 23 22 21 20 19 18 17 16 15

Photographs ©: Alamy Images: 29 (Biju), 15 top left (blickwinkel), 28 top (Danita
Delimont), 23 (Photoshot Holdings Ltd); Biosphoto/Olivier Born: 7, 27 top right,
31 bottom; Science Source: 8, 27 bottom (Adam Jones), 12 (B.G. Thomson),
4, 31 center top (Chris Mattison/FLPA), 15 bottom right (ER Degginger), 15 bottom left
(Karl H. Switak), 24 (Leonard Lee Rue III), 15 top right (Michael Lustbader),
28 center (Scott Camazine), 28 bottom (Tony Camacho); Superstock, Inc.: 19, 27
top left, 31 top (Animals Animals), 20, 31 center bottom (Biosphoto), 30 bottom (Jane
Sweeney/Jon Arnold Images), cover (Minden Pictures), 16 (Nomad), 3 top right,
11 (Roberta Olenick/All Canada Photos); Thinkstock: 30 top right (Anton Foltin),
3 top left (Eric Isselée), 30 top left (HappyToBeHomeless), 3 bottom (Steve Lenz).

Table of Contents

It's a Good Thing...

Snakes can look scary as they slither along the ground. Some can even be deadly. But it is a good thing there are snakes!

Snakes hunt rats and other pests that harm farm crops.

Snake **venom** can be used to make medicine.

A scientist collects venom from a cobra.

7

Snakes are also food for birds, foxes, raccoons, and other animals.

A blue heron catches
a water snake.

What Are Snakes?

A snake is a **reptile**. Reptiles are cold-blooded. They need the sun's heat to stay warm. Snakes go into the shade to cool down.

Most snakes live in warm areas. They are found in jungles, deserts, and forests. Some live in trees and water.

Lizards and turtles are reptiles, too.

scales

There are more than 2,700 kinds of snakes in the world.

Snakes do not have legs. But they can still slither, swim, and climb. A snake's **scales** and stomach muscles help it move. Its hard scales also keep its body safe.

FUN FACT!

Snakes never blink. That is because they do not have eyelids. Clear scales cover their eyes.

Snakes protect themselves in many ways. Green snakes can hide in trees. Brown snakes are hard to spot in sand. Some snakes use their bright colors to warn enemies to stay away. Others play dead until danger has passed.

FUN FACT!

Some snakes hiss to warn enemies to stay away. When a rattlesnake senses danger, it shakes its tail.

green tree python

green vine snake

Mojave Desert
sidewinder

northern black-tail
rattlesnake

A hognose snake eats a toad.

On the Hunt

Snakes hunt their food. They eat frogs, birds, mice, fish, and even other snakes.

Snakes do not see well. But they have a strong sense of smell. A snake flicks its tongue in and out to smell food.

A snake uses its teeth to hold **prey**, but not to chew it. All snakes swallow their prey whole.

Only some snakes use poison to kill their food. They have sharp teeth called fangs. When they bite, their venom flows into the prey's body.

Many snakes, like this Gaboon viper, stay completely still and then attack.

This African rock python wraps its body around its prey until it stops breathing.

Other snakes squeeze their prey to death. Big snakes, such as boas and pythons, eat large animals. They can stretch their mouths wide enough to swallow a whole pig, deer, or goat.

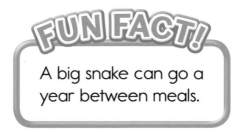

FUN FACT!

A big snake can go a year between meals.

How Snakes Grow

Most snakes lay eggs. Each baby has a special tooth to help break the egg. The tooth falls off soon after the snake hatches. Other snakes give birth to live young.

A green mamba baby pokes out of its egg.

Snakes, like this rattlesnake, shed their skin throughout their lives.

As snakes get bigger, their skin becomes tight and sheds. This is called molting. Snakes rub on trees or rocks to get the old skin off. New skin is underneath. The snake will continue to grow and shed its skin for the rest of its life.

FUN FACT!

The anaconda (an-uh-KON-duh) is the world's heaviest snake. It weighs about 550 pounds (250 kilograms). That's about as much as 11 kids! Anacondas live in South America's Amazon rain forest.

From helping farmers to providing food for animals, slithery, scaly snakes help us in many ways. It's a good thing there are snakes!

Snakes Are Good For...

...hunting pests that eat crops.

...providing venom for medicines.

...providing food for birds, toads, and other animals.

The longest snake is the **reticulated** (ri-TIK-yoo-lay-tid) **python** of Southeast Asia. It can be as long as a school bus.

The smallest snake in the world is the **thread snake**. It is about the size of an earthworm.

A **desert sidewinder** snake throws its body sideways to move.

Feature Fun

The **king cobra** of Southeast Asia is the world's longest venomous snake. One bite can kill an elephant. A cobra raises its head and spreads its hood to look big and scary.

RIDDLES

Q. What is a snake's favorite subject?

A. *Hiss-tory!*

Q. How do you measure a snake?

A. *In inches. They don't have feet!*

Creature Feature Fun

Which habitat is right for snakes?

A

B

Answer: B. Snakes like warm areas, such as this desert.

Protecting Snakes

People can be a threat to snakes. Snakes lose their homes when people cut down trees or build homes. Some people hunt snakes for their skins or because they are afraid of them. Most snakes do not hurt people. But you should leave them alone. Snakes bite to protect themselves from danger.

Glossary

prey (PRAY): animals hunted by other animals

reptile (REP-tile): cold-blooded animal with a body temperature that is the same as the air around it

scales (SKALES): thin, hard pieces of skin that cover a snake's body

venom (VEN-uhm): poison from a snake that comes through its fangs

Index

Facts for Now

Visit this Scholastic Web site for more information on snakes:
www.factsfornow.scholastic.com
Enter the keyword **Snakes**

About the Author

Lisa M. Herrington writes books and articles for kids. She finds snakes fascinating. Lisa lives in Trumbull, Connecticut, with her husband, Ryan, and daughter, Caroline.